THE SUMMER OF THE SWANS

by
Betsy Byars

D1713046

Teacher Guide

Written by:
Jean Jamieson

> **Note**
> The Puffin Books paperback edition was used to prepare this teacher guide. The page references may differ in the hardcover or other paperback editions.

ISBN 1-56137-114-9

To order, contact your local
school supply store, or—

Novel Units, Inc.
P.O. Box 791610
San Antonio, TX 78279

Table of Contents

Skills and Strategies

Thinking
> Brainstorming, classifying
> and categorizing, evaluating,
> analyzing details

Comprehension
> Sequencing, comparison/
> contrast, using reference
> materials, inference

Writing
> Letter, advice column,
> descriptive, figures of speech

Vocabulary
> Antonyms/synonyms, word
> maps, analogies

Listening/Speaking
> Participation in discussion,
> participation in dramatic
> activities

Literary Elements
> Character, setting, plot
> development

Summary of The Summer of the Swans
Sara's fourteenth summer is not a happy one. She feels that no one understands her, she's not pretty, and she has to watch her retarded brother, Charlie, during the day. Sara takes Charlie to watch the swans, and that night he leaves the house to go to find them. Charlie is soon lost. Unable to speak, and afraid of people, he wanders deeper and deeper into the woods. From this troublesome time, Sara learns what it means to really care about someone else.

About the Author:
Betsy Cromer Byars was born August 7, 1928, in Charlotte, North Carolina. She married Edward Ford Byars, a professor of engineering, June 24, 1950. They have four children, Laurie, Betsy Ann, Nan, and Guy. She attended Furman University, 1946-48; Queens College, B.A. in 1950.

Byars had a happy childhood. Her father worked at a small cotton mill, so brought home free cloth, enabling Byars to learn to sew at an early age. "I sewed fast, without patterns, and with great hope and determination, and that is approximately the same way that I write."

When she went to college, she majored in math, for that is what her father wanted her to do, and what her sister had done before her. "I had discovered early in life that things were easier all around if I lived up to my father's expectations." However, calculus was the determinant that made her go to her father to tell him that she could not be a mathematician. She switched her major to English, and married after graduation so that her only writing during the next few years was of letters and shopping lists. When her husband went back to school to study for his doctorate, Byars started her creative writing. His doctorate completed, Byars and her family moved to West Virginia, where her children's novels were written.

Byars was awarded the Newbery Medal for *The Summer of the Swans* in 1971. Her books have been translated into nine languages, and many have been dramatized on national television. She has said, "There is no activity in my life which has brought me more pleasure than my writing."

Newbery Medal:
The medal is named for eighteenth-century British bookseller John Newbery, the first bookseller and publisher to make a specialty of children's books. It is awarded annually by the Association For Library Service To Children, a division of the American Library Association, to the author of The Most Distinguished Contribution To American Literature For Children. (See Teacher Information/John Newbery.)

Note:
Please be selective, and use discretion when choosing the activities that you will do with this unit. It is not intended that everything be done, but that discretionary choices made are most appropriate for your use and group of children. A wide range has been provided, so that individuals as well as groups may benefit from these selections.

To the Teacher:
Before starting this unit of study, it is recommended that you make arrangements to have experts in the field of mental retardation ready to come in to speak to the children in your group. Your own school district, neighboring high schools, local agencies, etc., are some sources for information and help. Local library personnel could be of assistance in locating books about children with mental retardation, as well as informational books on various reading levels.

You may also wish to contact the following agencies, and/or others:

Administration on Developmental Disabilities
Department of Health and Human Services
200 Independence Avenue SW
Washington, DC 20201

Association for Retarded Citizens
P.O. Box 6109
Arlington, TX 76006

Council for Exceptional Children
1920 Association Drive
Reston, VA 22091

Mainstream
1200 15th Street NW, Suite 403
Washington, DC 20005

National Down's Syndrome Society
141 Fifth Avenue
New York, New York 10010

Special Olympics
1350 New York Avenue NW
Suite 500
Washington, DC 20005

Initiating Activities:
1. Kaleidoscope: Collect different kaleidoscopes, and have them placed in easy access areas in the room. Cut some large regular polygon shapes out of colored plastic, and have those hanging in the room. (Cut the shapes in proportionate sizes, so that, when taken down, they will fit together to make a tessellated design, similar to one that might be seen in a kaleidoscope.)

   When ready to start the activity, have the children look through the kaleidoscopes, and describe what they see. What causes the changes in the design? Does anyone know how a kaleidoscope is made? Discuss kaleidoscopes. (The kaleidoscope works on the principle of multiple reflection. Two glass plates inside serve as mirrors. They go down the entire length of the side, and slant toward each other. At the far end of the kaleidoscope are two more plates, one made of clear glass, and the other of ground glass. The clear glass is closer to the eyehole. Pieces of colored beads and glass are placed between the plates. The beads and glass are reflected in the mirrors. The ground glass throws the reflections in many directions, and patterns are formed. When the viewer turns the kaleidoscope, the colored beads and glass shift, and the patterns change. Source: *The World Book Encyclopedia*, 1991.)

In the novel, one of the characters refers to her life as, "...a huge kaleidoscope." What do you think that she means by that statement?

2. Tolerance: Place within easy access to the children the materials that you have collected from the agencies contacted, as well as library books, etc. When ready to start this activity, read to the children the poem "Were You Ever Fat Like Me?" found on page 52 of the book *If You're Not Here, Please Raise Your Hand*. (See Bibliography, Dakos.) Discuss differences, and the way in which children who are perceived to be different from others are treated. (You may wish to use additional selections from this book of poetry.)

Turn to page 52 of *The Summer of the Swans*, and read to the children the second sentence of the paragraph starting about ¼ of the page down, "Charlie was not..." Preface the reading by telling the children that Charlie is 10 years old when this story takes place. Read, "When he was three..."

Explain to the children that, because of this brain damage, we find out that Charlie does things, and learns, in a way that may not be the same as his sisters. Does this make Charlie any less of a human being? Discuss.

Charlie's difference from his sisters may be significant, but isn't each one of us different from the other? Each person is unique. It is important to accept that uniqueness, and to appreciate the human being first.

For ideas and strategies for the teaching of tolerance, write for a free copy of *Teaching Tolerance*. Source: Teaching Tolerance, 400 Washington Avenue, Montgomery, Alabama 36104.

Bulletin Board Ideas:

1. Kaleidoscope: Cover the bulletin board with plain background paper. Place on the background paper one tessellated design made from colored paper regular polygon shapes. (It is suggested that you use as examples the pattern block shapes of the hexagon, trapezoid, diamond, and triangle.) Have volunteers make additional shapes to place on the bulletin board. (See Supplementary Activities/Symmetry.)

2. Tolerance: Cover the bulletin board with plain background paper. Add a caption. (For example: "We share a world. For all our differences of politics, race, economics,

abilities, culture, and language, we share one world. To be tolerant is to welcome the differences and delight in the sharing.")

Prereading Activity:
Look at the picture on the cover of the book. What does the artist tell the reader about the story, and about two of the characters? Discuss.

The artist, Ted CoConis, gives his interpretation of the story by showing physical characteristics of people, places, and things. However, he does not tell the reader everything. The author tells the reader, on page 22, that Charlie, pictured on the cover, is "retarded." What does the word "retarded" mean to you? Brainstorm. Record replies made by students.

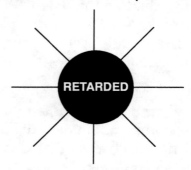

Come to a consensus as to what "retarded" means. Use a word map to record the definition.

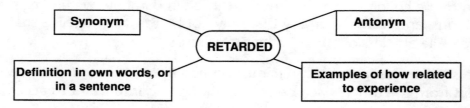

Invite the first guest speaker to come give background information to the children in the group. Have out materials and books on the subject, so that the children may investigate further.

Recommended Procedure:
It is recommended that this book be read one chapter at a time, using the DRTA, Directed Reading Thinking Activity, Method. This technique involves reading a chapter at a time, and then predicting what will happen next by making good guesses based on what has already occurred in the story. The predictions are recorded, and verified after the subsequent reading has taken place.

You may wish to have students show knowledge of words in the vocabulary before reading the chapter by writing simple definitions in their own words. After reading, the students may need to redefine the words by referring to the text and/or a dictionary.

Chapter 1—Pages 9-16

Vocabulary:

peasant 9   inscrutable 10   pathetic 10
kaleidoscope 13

Vocabulary Activity:
Use all four words in the same sentence. Make an illustration for the sentence.

Discussion Questions and Activities:

1. Who are the characters introduced in the first chapter? *(Sara Godfrey, Boysie—the dog, Wanda Godfrey, aunt, Charlie Godfrey)*

2. What are the physical imperfections of Sara and Wanda? *(Pages 10-11, Sara has big feet, and Wanda has "perfectly terrible hands," and stubby fingers.)*

3. Boysie, the dog, is 84 years old, in people age. *(page 10)* How old is that in dog age? How do you know? *(Divide 84 by 7 to find out Boysie's dog age, which is 12.)*

4. Is Sara enjoying the summer? *(No)* Sara compares the summer to a toy and a playground activity. What are they? *(page 13, kaleidoscope; page 16, seesaw)* Why do you think that she uses these particular things? Do you think that these are two things that most people can relate to, and have experienced? (See Postreading Activity #1 and Postreading Activity #2.)

5. Have you noticed anything special about Charlie? *(Pages 13-16, Charlie has trouble putting the candy back on the lollipop stick.)* Start an attribute web for Charlie. Keep it in view, and add to it as more is learned about him. What do others say about him? say to him? think of him? How do others treat him? act toward him? What is his speech, his behavior like? (See page 43 of this guide.)

Postreading Activities:

1. Compare Sara's bad summer to something other than a kaleidoscope or seesaw.

2. Write a descriptive paragraph or poem about how you think that Sara is feeling about the summer. For example:

Enveloped by the darkness inside,
I am surrounded by the brightly colored glass.
The kaleidoscope of life is turned,
And from the known I must pass.

Pass into the uncertain, the who knows what?
I stumble and am rendered unsteady,
Unshapely, and distorted to view.
Yet an eye peers in, whether or not I am ready.

3. Start a story map. What do you think that the problem is? What is the goal? Add to the story map as the story evolves. (See page 42 of this guide.)

4. Start attribute webs for Sara and Wanda. Add to them as the story evolves. (See page 43 of this guide.)

5. Make predictions as to what this story might be about. Record the predictions for verification as more of the story is read.

Chapter 2—Pages 17-19

Vocabulary:

illusion 18   silhouette 19

Vocabulary Activity:

Silhouette: A likeness cut from dark material and mounted on a light background, or one sketched in outline and solidly colored in. Make a silhouette of someone or something.

Discussion Questions and Activities:
1. What additional information are we given about Charlie? *(Pages 17-19, Charlie has a nervous habit of moving his feet back and forth on the steps. Charlie does not talk. Charlie does not know how to make a tent with a blanket over a clothesline. Charlie is small in size for being 10 years old.)*

2. On page 19 the author tells us that, although Sara was talking about the summer, "He [Charlie] could tell from the tone of her voice that she was not really talking to him at all." Has that ever happened to you? Would you like to tell us about it? Have you ever talked to someone, and felt that the person was not listening to you? What happened in this case? How did you feel about it?

Postreading Activities:
1. Charlie seems to be able to understand what is said to him, even though he does not speak. Many mentally retarded people can be taught to use sign language, so that they are able to communicate with others. Start to learn sign language. (If you are not comfortable teaching it to the children, invite a volunteer to come in to teach it. There are also videocassettes available for that purpose. See Bibliography/Sign Language and Audio-Visual Bibliography/Sign Language.) You may wish to read the short book *We Laugh, We Love, We Cry* to the children. It is about two young mentally retarded sisters who learn sign language. (See Bibliography/Mental Retardation/Bergman.)

2. Write out directions for making a tent out of a blanket hung over a clothesline. Make an illustration to go with the directions.

Chapter 3—Pages 20-23

Vocabulary:

grimace 20   emphatically 21   rhododendron 22

Vocabulary Activity:

Think of as many words as you can that begin with the same letter/sound as *rhododendron.*
Make a list. Using the word *rhododendron,* and two others from the list, make a tongue
twister. Try to say the three words as fast as you can four times. As you get good at it, add
another word to the tongue twister. Continue until you have at least five words to repeat.

Resplendent Red Rhododendron
Radiant Resplendent Red Rhododendron
Really Radiant Resplendent Red Rhododendron

Discussion Questions and Activities:

1. Why do the children live with their Aunt Willie? *(Page 20, They live with their Aunt Willie because their mother died six years previously.)*

2. After reading this chapter, do you think that there is more than one problem? What might the problems in the story be? *(For example: Charlie is retarded. Wanda and Sara do not seem to get along. The children live with their Aunt Willie.)*

3. Aunt Willie is opposed to Wanda riding on a motor scooter, which she refers to as a motorcycle. Why to you think that she feels as she does? (See Postreading Activity #1.)

4. How do you think that the people in the story relate to one another? Do they listen to one another? Do they seem to care about one another?

5. What do you think that Wanda means when she says that Charlie is everybody's problem? *(page 23)* How would you explain that statement?

Postreading Activities:

1. List the arguments for and against riding on the motor scooter.

For	Against

2. Make a prediction. What do you think will happen next?

Chapter 4—Pages 24-30

Vocabulary:

uneventful 24	indignation 25	matador 25
sidesaddle 27	spigot 27	pivoting 27

Vocabulary Activity:

Use each set of three words in one sentence.

Uneventful—matador—sidesaddle
Indignation—spigot—matador
Matador—indignation—uneventful

Discussion Questions and Activities:

1. Aunt Willie talks to Sara, who insists that "Wanda is a hundred times prettier than I am" *(page 28)*, and tells her, "It's not how you look that's important..." *(page 29)* How does Sara feel about that statement? Do you agree or disagree with Aunt Willie? Why?

2. Sara decides to go to see the swans at the lake. Aunt Willie asks Charlie if he would like to go with Sara. *(page 30)* How does Sara feel about this inclusion of Charlie? Why do you think that she feels as she does? Did Aunt Willie consult Sara first? What might have helped the situation?

3. Sara complains to Aunt Willie, on page 30, that she never gets to do anything alone. She has to take Charlie everywhere. She has him all day and Wanda all night. Sara adds that, in the whole house, she has but one drawer to herself. Role play the scene in which Aunt Willie and Sara are holding this conversation on the bottom of page 29 and all of page 30. Express how Sara is feeling by the way in which the words are said.

Postreading Activities:

1. What is the goal in this story? How is a goal different from a problem? Write one sentence about the goal, and one sentence about the problem.

2. Add on to the attribute webs. Start one for Aunt Willie.

3. Make some predictions as to what will happen next.

Chapter 5—Pages 31-34

Vocabulary:

theme 31	disappointment 33

Vocabulary Activity:
How many words can you make from the letters in the word *disappointment* in five minutes? *(Here are some: point, pin, mint, men, man, tan, pan, sand, pen, sap, tap, map, nap, pat, sat, mat, stint, saint, dip, sip, tip, nip, pip, ten, mean...)*

Discussion Questions and Activities:
1. Sara talks to Charlie about her problems with her sister and her looks. *(page 31)* Charlie can't talk and tell Sara what he feels and believes about these things. What would you tell Sara? Do you believe that looks are the most important thing in the world? Why or why not?

2. Do you think that the teacher gave Sara a **D** because of <u>what</u> she said about looks, or the <u>way</u> in which she said it? Do you think that makes a difference? Do you think that it should? *(Opinion—answers will vary.)*

3. Where does this story take place? *(page 32, West Virginia, in the strip mining country)* (See Postreading Activity #1.)

Postreading Activities:
1. Do some research. Find out more about West Virginia. What are the economic conditions in that state at the present time? (See Teacher Information section at the back of this guide.)

2. The Appalachian Trail goes through the eastern most corner of West Virginia. Find out more about the historic significance of the area in which this occurs. *(Civil War)*

3. Sara tells Charlie to sit on the step, and not to move from there. Do you think that Charlie will do as he is told? Make a prediction.

Chapter 6—Pages 35-39

Vocabulary:
      rhythmic 37   obediently 37

Vocabulary Activity:
The rhythmic ticking of his watch seemed to soothe Charlie. Clap out the rhythm of the ticking of the clock, your watch, etc. If available, play a metronome at several different settings, and clap to the rhythm.

Discussion Questions and Activities:
1. This chapter tells more about Charlie. What does he like? dislike? *(For example: He likes the ticking of his watch. He dislikes being left alone.)*

2. Why is Charlie's watch so important to him? *(Page 35, The watch gives him great plea-sure. He likes to listen to it, and to watch the small red hand move around the dial.)*

Postreading Activities:
1. Go to the library. Get some books about swans and ducks. Compare the swans, as pictured on the cover of the book, to mallard ducks. Use a T-Diagram for the comparison. For example:

	DUCKS	SWANS
Color		
Size		
Habitat		
Food		

2. We are told, on page 38, that the children cut across a field on their way to the pond. Why do you think that they do this? Do you think that this fact is important to the story? Why? Why not?

Chapter 7—Pages 40-46

Vocabulary:
incredible 40   awkwardly 41

Vocabulary Activity:
Using the form given, make word maps for the two vocabulary words.

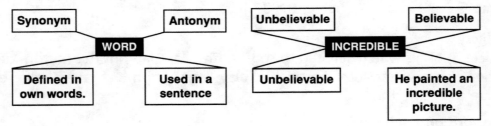

Discussion Questions and Activities:
1. Why is Sara so unhappy? *(Page 46, "She was filled with a discontent, an anger about herself, her life, her family, that made her think she would never be content again.")*

2. What does Sara do, to finally get Charlie to agree to go home? *(Page 46, She agrees to stay five more minutes, and shows Charlie the time on the watch that they will have to leave.)*

Postreading Activities:
1. Play some music from the ballet *Swan Lake* while the children illustrate the scene of the swans on the pond. Have different media available for use, such as craypas, chalk, watercolors, tempera paint, charcoal, finger-paint, etc. (See Audio-Visual Bibliography, Tchaikovsky.)

2. Have different versions of the story of Swan Lake available for the children to read. (See Teacher Information/Swan Lake, and Bibliography/Swan Lake.)

Chapter 8—Pages 47-53

Vocabulary:

affected 48	dedicate 51	tormented 52
persist 53		

Vocabulary Activity:
Read the following sentences. Fill in each blank with a vocabulary word.

1. Frank is going to _____a song to Wanda. *(dedicate)*

2. Charlie will _____in kicking the wall in his bedroom. *(persist)*

3. Sara thinks that Frank is _____because he calls Wanda Little One. *(affected)*

4. Charlie had an illness with a high fever that _____his body. *(tormented)*

Discussion Questions and Activities:
1. What words might Sara use to describe herself? *(Page 49, "I'm not anything. I'm not cute, and I'm not pretty, and I'm not a good dancer, and I'm not smart, and I'm not popular. I'm not anything.")*

2. Can you help Sara? Role play a situation in which one child takes the part of Sara, and a partner is the school counselor. Switch roles after a predetermined amount of time. (See Postreading Activity #1.)

Postreading Activities:
1. Write a letter to an advice columnist in the local paper. You may take the role of Sara, or you may take a different part and have different problems. Explain your problem(s) to the columnist, and ask for some specific advice.

2. Take the role of the newspaper columnist, and give a reply to a specific problem. Be sure that the problem is stated before giving advice.

Chapter 9—Pages 54-60

Prereading Prediction:
Charlie can't sleep. What might he do? List responses.

Vocabulary:

gross 55	puce 55	linoleumed 58

Vocabulary Activity:
Describe what you *think* the color puce would look like. *(Puce: Color that is deep red to dark grayish purple.)* Mix some watercolor paint or tempera paint, to achieve the color that you describe.

Discussion Questions and Activities:
1. Why is Charlie especially disturbed and unable to sleep on this particular night? *(Page 54, A button is missing from his pajamas.)*

2. Charlie shows the place where the button belongs to Aunt Willie. Why doesn't she fix it for Charlie? *(Page 54, Aunt Willie is busy watching a game show on television.)*

3. Why doesn't Sara help Charlie? *(Page 55, Sara is busy dyeing her orange shoes.)* What happens when Sara tries to dye her orange shoes baby blue? *(Page 55, The shoes are colored puce.)* Do you think that you would like to wear puce-colored shoes? Why? Why not?

4. Charlie is so upset by the missing button, that he pulls at the empty buttonhole. What eventually happens? *(Page 56, He tears the whole front of his pajama top, and it hangs open. He must hold the jacket closed with his hands.)*

5. Why does Charlie like the swans so much? *(Page 56, "The memory of their soft smoothness in the water came to him and warmed him"; page 57, "The beauty of them, the whiteness, the softness, the silent splendor had impressed him greatly...")*

6. What does Charlie do? *(Page 59, Charlie leaves the house, to go to look for the swans.)*

Postreading Activities:
1. The author tells us, on page 59, that Charlie seems to belong to the silent world of the night. Read some poetry that describes the night, and/or something happening during the night. Make up a class poem about the night. Allow the children to create their own poetry. (See Bibliography, Livingston, Merriam, dePaola, Prelutsky.)

2. Make a prediction. What will happen to Charlie? Record predictions.

Chapter 10—Pages 61-64

Vocabulary:

scanned 61   briers* 61   hopelessness 64

This is the spelling used by the author throughout this book. Briars is also acceptable.

Vocabulary Activity:
Describe the feeling of *hopelessness*.

Discussion Questions and Activities:
1. Charlie is lost and afraid. List some of the words and/or phrases that describe how he feels. Is the author effective in describing Charlie's terror? For example:

   (Page 61): "terribly frightened"; "ran...thrashing at weeds"; "like a wild animal caught in a maze"; "briers stung his face and arms..."

   (Page 62): "thrashed his arms out wildly"; "staggered on"; "ran blindly"; "stumbling over bushes"; "kicking at unseen rocks"; "gasping for breath"; "rasping sound of Charlie's own breathing..."

   (Page 64): "struggling"; "gripped by hopelessness"; "to cry without sound"; "had wanted something but could not remember what..."

2. Have you ever been lost? Describe for us the feelings that you experienced. How did you react? List all of the words and/or phrases that describe how you felt. Use this list to write a paragraph telling of your feelings. Share this paragraph with a classmate.

Postreading Activities:
1. Make a prediction. How do you think that the family members will react to Charlie's disappearance?

2. Play some classical music for the children as they make illustrations to depict the feelings experienced by Charlie. Have available for use a large selection of materials, such as: craypas, chalk, charcoal, watercolors, tempera paint, colored tissue paper, glue, finger paint, etc.

Chapter 11—Pages 65-73

Vocabulary:

chide 68   posse 71

Vocabulary Activity:
Look up the definition of both words in the dictionary. Use the words in sentences. Illustrate one of the sentences.

Discussion Questions and Activities:

1. When Sara gets up in the morning, she has two big worries. What are they? *(page 65, her hair and her shoes)* What makes this change? *(Page 69, Charlie is missing.)*

2. Why isn't Sara worried at first? *(Page 69, Sara is sure that Charlie has gone to see the swans.)* Is Charlie at the pond? *(no)*

Postreading Activities:

1. Make a class list of suggested places for Sara and Mary to look for Charlie. Each child tells why that suggestion was made.

2. Make a prediction. Will Charlie be found? Will he be all right?

Chapter 12—Pages 74-80

Vocabulary:

grudgingly 75	agitation 75	ravines 77
elongated 77	revenge 79	

Vocabulary Activity:

Complete the following analogies, using words from the vocabulary list. Sample: COLD is to HOT as _____ is to WHITE. *(BLACK)*

1. NICE is to LIKABLE as _____ is to RELUCTANTLY. *(GRUDGINGLY)*

2. HAPPY is to GLAD as _____ is to RETALIATION. *(REVENGE)*

3. NIGHT is to DAY as _____ is to CALM. *(AGITATION)*

4. GOODBYE is to FAREWELL as _____ is to STRETCHED. *(ELONGATED)*

Discussion Questions and Activities:

1. Why is Aunt Willie so upset about Charlie's disappearance? *(Page 76, Aunt Willie had promised Charlie's mother that she would look after him all of her life. She feels guilty because she has neglected Charlie to watch television.)* (See Postreading Activity #1.)

2. Charlie has drawn a picture of himself. How does the drawing remind Sara of Charlie? *(Page 77, "...something about the picture, the smallness, the unfinished quality, made it look somehow very much like Charlie.")*

3. We meet Joe Melby for the first time in this chapter. *(page 79)* Why is he important in this chapter? *(Sara says that Joe stole Charlie's watch. Aunt Willie says that the watch was lost, and that Joe found and returned it.)*

4. We find out more about Sara's character in this chapter. What do we learn? *(Pages 79-80, Sara seeks revenge against Joe, and she holds a grudge against Gretchen Wyant because Gretchen called Charlie a "retard.")* What brought out these feelings in Sara? *(Sara thinks that Joe and Gretchen do not treat Charlie in the right way. She does it out of her feelings for him.)* Discuss.

Postreading Activities:
1. Have you ever neglected doing something because you watched television instead? How important is television to you? Could you go for a day without watching it? Two days? How long do you think that you could do without television? Are you willing to try to find out? Let us know how you do!

2. Draw a picture of yourself. Write a paragraph about yourself to go with the picture. Is it hard to draw a picture or to write a description of yourself? List class responses.

Chapter 13—Pages 81-87

Vocabulary:

remoteness 82   sustain 83

Vocabulary Activity:

In this chapter, the *remoteness* of the children's father is introduced. Describe some kinds of behavior, or incidents, that would illustrate this.

Discussion Questions and Activities:
1. What are some of the changes that have occurred in Sara's father since her mother's death? *(Pages 82-83, The father has become remote. He no longer laughs. He has to work in Ohio, so rarely spends time with his family. He never starts a conversation.)*

2. What does Sara's father decide to do when told that Charlie is missing? *(Page 84, He is going to call back after work, and will come at that time if it is necessary.)* What does Sara think that her father should do? *(From the way that she is reacting, it is implied that Sara does not approve of her father's behavior. It is assumed that she would like him to come right away.)* (See Postreading Activity #1.)

Postreading Activities:
1. Think of the reasons for and against Sara's father coming to West Virginia just as soon as he is told that Charlie is missing. List class responses.

Reasons For	Reasons Against
This is a serious matter.	Charlie might be found at any minute.
Lots of help is needed.	Father would lose a day's pay.
It is a sign that the father cares about Charlie.	It is a long drive.

2. Create a poster regarding Charlie and his disappearance. What is the purpose of your poster? Knowing that, what will you include, so that the poster will be helpful? Put the poster on display in the room or hall.

Chapter 14—Pages 88-92

Vocabulary:

accusation 89   incident 89   exaggerated 91

Vocabulary Activity:

Exaggerate: To make something greater than it actually is; magnify beyond the truth; to increase to an abnormal degree. Give an example of *exaggeration.* You may decide to write a sentence, a paragraph, do something that is exaggerated, or demonstrate the word and its meaning in some other way.

Discussion Questions and Activities:
1. Why doesn't Sara want Joe's help in finding Charlie? *(Page 89, Sara thinks that Joe had previously stolen Charlie's watch. "Anybody who would steal a little boy's watch... is somebody whose help I can very well do without.")* Does this accusation stop Joe from helping? *(No; page 90, Joe tells Sara that he returned the watch to Charlie. He did not take it.)* (See Postreading Activity #1.)

2. Why do you think that Sara is crying? *(Page 91, Opinion—answers will vary.)*

Postreading Activities:
1. How would you have accepted Joe's offer of help? Role play different ways of giving and accepting help with a partner. Switch roles.

2. The word *blue* is sometimes used to mean gloomy or depressed. This may be the way that Sara is feeling at this time. Use the color blue to depict the feeling *blue.* You may wish to use a variety of materials, and make a collage that is made entirely of things that are different shades of blue in color. You may decide to use mixed media, such as paint and tissue paper, chalk and charcoal, craypas and ink, etc.

Chapter 15—Pages 93-97

Discussion Questions and Activities:
1. How does Sara find out the real story regarding Charlie's watch? *(Mary tells Sara the story. It is on page 95. Ask someone to summarize what happened to the watch.)*

2. Why hasn't Mary told this to Sara before? *(Page 96, Mary tells Sara that she just found out about it at lunch. "For four months my mother has known all about this thing and never mentioned it because she said it was one of those things best forgotten.")*

Postreading Activities:

1. On page 97 there is a radio description of Charlie. What other points could you add?

2. If you have already made the poster of Charlie, (see Chapter 13), write a description of Charlie for the newspaper.

Chapter 16—Pages 98-107

Vocabulary:

nauseated 101   cicadas 103   indestructible 106
impetuously 107

Vocabulary Activity:

Match up the antonyms with vocabulary words.

<u>Antonym</u>	<u>Vocabulary Word</u>
breakable	*(indestructible)*
well	*(nauseated)*
thoughtfully	*(impetuously)*

Discussion Questions and Activities:

1. Mary goes with Sara, to look for Charlie. However, what is Mary most interested in? *(Page 98, Mary is most interested in going to Bennie Hoffman's party.)*

2. Sara thinks that Aunt Willie is worried about Charlie going into the old mine because of something that happened in the past. What was that? *(Page 99, Aunt Willie's uncle and brother were killed in that coal mine.)* Does Sara agree with her? *(Page 99, No; she thinks that it is too cold and dark, and scary for Charlie.)* (See Postreading Activity #1.)

3. What does Joe find? *(Page 102, Joe finds a brown felt slipper. It is Charlie's!)* What other clue do the children have that Charlie might have come that way? *(Page 102, Joe finds out that Mr. Aker's dogs were barking the night before, and he thought that someone was prowling around.)* What does Mary volunteer to do? *(Page 103, Mary volunteers to go to the gas station to tell the people who are organizing the search that Charlie is in the woods, not in the mine.)*

4. Sara and Joe find that they have some things in common. What are they? *(Pages 106-107, They both received check marks on their report cards in grammar-school for "Does not accept criticism constructively," and "Acts impetuously and without consideration for others.")* Do you notice a change in the relationship between these two story characters at this time? What do you think is happening?

Postreading Activities:
1. Most of us are frightened about something. Fear is an emotional warning system. What frightens you? Discuss. (Make sure that the children notice that everyone has fears. They are not alone! See Supplementary Activities/Fear.)

2. Sara has a hard time telling Joe that she is sorry about the "Fink" sign, and about accusing him of stealing the watch. Have you ever had a hard time apologizing? How did you do it? Tell a classmate the story, and role play how you said that you were sorry.

Chapter 17—Pages 108-111

Vocabulary:

ravine 108	roused 108	finality 109
flailing 111	anguish 111	

Vocabulary Activities:
Anguish: An agonizing physical or mental pain; torment, torture. What kinds of occurrences do you think would bring on a feeling of *anguish*? Discuss.

Discussion Questions and Activities:
1. How did you feel when you read this chapter? List responses.

2. Pick out the best, most effective sentence in this chapter. Why do you think that this is a great sentence? (See Postreading Activity #1.)

Postreading Activities:
1. Illustrate the feeling that you have when reading the sentence that you have chosen.

2. Choose a song or a poem that illustrates the feeling that you have when reading the sentence that you have chosen. Share your choice(s) with others.

Chapter 18—Pages 112-116

Vocabulary:

tremulous 112	dialogue 114	compulsion 114

Vocabulary Activity:
Tremulous: Vibrating or quivering. The word *tremulous* is used in this chapter to describe the whistle of a bird. Demonstrate how this would sound.

Discussion Questions and Activities:
1. Sara compares the long climb to the top of the hill in two different ways. What are they? (*Page 114, She compares the climb to a slow bicycle race that she won; pages 115-116, she compares Joe's remark, "We're almost there," [the top of the hill], to the dentist's*

remark, *"I'm almost through drilling."*) Are these meaningful comparisons to you? (See Postreading Activity #1.)

2. How do you think that Sara feels at the close of this chapter? *(Opinion—answers will vary.)*

Postreading Activities:
1. Make your own comparisons for the long, hard climb to the top of the hill.

2. The author creates pictures in the reader's mind by using literary imagery. Find examples of similes, metaphors, and/or personification in this book. For example: (A **simile** uses the words <u>like</u> or <u>as</u> to compare two very different things. A **metaphor** suggests a comparison by saying one thing is another <u>without using like or as</u>. **Personification** is used when a writer gives human characteristics to an animal or an object.)

(Page 25)	"She held the dish towel in front of her, like a matador..."
(Page 27)	"Her scream, shrill as a bird's cry..."
(Page 117)	"...valley...a tiny finger of civilization..."
(Page 125)	"...shoes slapping the ground like rubber paddles..."
(Page 125)	"...crying like the sound of a cricket..."
(Page 126)	"...arms gripped her like steel..."
(Page 134)	"...ran like a ball rolling downhill..."

3. Make up two examples of your own, using similes, metaphors, and/or personification.

Chapter 19—Pages 117-120

Discussion Question and Activity:
What does Sara conclude about her worries and concerns of the summer? *(Page 119, That they were unimportant. "I have cried over myself a hundred times this summer, she thought, I have wept over my big feet and my skinny legs and my nose, I have cried over my stupid shoes, and now when I have a true sadness there are no tears left.")* Why do you think that there are "no tears left"?

Postreading Activity:
On page 120 the author tells us that Sara "sank to the ground and sat with her head bent over her knees." We can imagine how Sara is feeling when doing this. There are times when words do not have to be spoken in order for us to know how others are feeling. Show us how you feel today. Show us other feelings, if you wish. Describe the situation.

Chapter 20—Pages 121-123

Discussion Question and Activity:
What is important to Charlie, to keep him feeling safe and well? *(Page 122, Strict routine is*

important, as well as the same foods, bed, furniture in the same place, the same seat on the school bus, and the same class procedure.) Do you feel better when you know what to expect? What change in your routine bothers you the most?

Postreading Activity:
Reread Charlie's awakening, starting with, "The first thing..." on page 122. Think of something, like Aunt Willie's cigar box, that is important to you. Close your eyes. What's in there? Dictate a description of your treasure to a partner. Switch roles. What is a treasure?

Chapter 21—Pages 124-129

Vocabulary:
cascade 125   disbelief 126

Discussion Questions and Activities:
1. On pages 124 and 125 the author describes Sara's feelings as she goes to Charlie. Read these pages once again, and choose the descriptive part that you like the best. Why is this your choice?

2. How does Joe demonstrate that he, too, understands Charlie? *(Page 129, Charlie's watch is broken, so Joe puts his own watch on Charlie's arm, since a watch is important to Charlie.)*

Postreading Activity:
The author writes, on page 126, "He [Charlie] opened his eyes and as he saw Sara a strange expression came over his face, an expression of wonder and joy and disbelief, and Sara knew that if she lived to be a hundred no one would ever look at her quite that way again." How does this make you feel? Discuss.

Chapter 22—Pages 130-136

Discussion Questions and Activities:
1. What do you think that Aunt Willie is referring to when she says on page 134, "...may none of you ever lose anybody in the woods or in the mine or anywhere"? *(She is probably referring to Charlie being lost in the woods, and the deaths of her uncle and brother in the coal mine.)*

2. Why do you think that Sara accepted Joe's invitation to he party? *(Opinion—answers will vary.)* Would you have accepted an invitation to a party after such a day? Why? Why not?

Postreading Activities:
How does Sara change in the novel? Is this believable? Select six adjectives that best describe

Sara at the beginning of the novel. Choose another six that describe her at the close of the book. Compare your list with that of a classmate.

Chapter 23—Pages 137-142

Discussion Questions and Activities:

1. Why do you think that Sara keeps trying to avoid talking to her father when he calls and she answers the telephone? *(Page 139, Opinion—answers will vary.)*

2. What do you think that the role of the father is in this novel? Do you think that it is significant that he does not appear at home during the novel? (See Postreading Activity #1.)

3. Sara sees life, "...as a series of huge, uneven steps..." What does she see her father doing? Where is Charlie? What has Sara learned about herself and about life on this difficult day? *(Page 140, Her father is sitting at the bottom of some steps, not trying to go further. Charlie is on a flight of small, difficult steps. She has come out of the shadows, and could go as high as the sky.)*

Postreading Activities:

1. Change the ending of the novel by having the father come home the weekend following this incident. What will happen? Will Charlie's misadventure change the father in any way?

2. Choose one incident in the novel that had an effect on one or more of the characters, such as Aunt Willie's decision to ride on the motor scooter. Change her decision, thereby also changing the outcome. Write about the changes that would have occurred in the story if you change a decision made by a character.

   Decisive Plots: In literature, the plot often is carried along by the causes and effects of decisions made by characters in the story. Had the character made an alternate decision, the plot would have turned in a different direction. Even small decisions can bring about later events. The following diagram may be used to describe two situations in which decisions had to be made, what the decision was in the novel, and what alternative decision could have been made. Discuss the results of the decision. Write the changes in the plot that would have resulted, had the alternative decision been made.

   Decision in Novel:_____   Results:_____
   Situation:_____   Plot Changes: _____
   Alternative:_____   Results:_____

   Decision in Novel:_____   Results:_____
   Situation:_____   Plot Changes: _____
   Alternative:_____   Results:_____

Supplementary Activities

1. Fear: Create a poem that tells of some of your fears.

    Creepy, crawly things,
    And dark and creaky places.
    Monsters lurking here and there
    With green and ghoulish faces.

    Making an oral report,
    Or standing before a group.
    These scary, frightful things
    Just throw me for a loop.

    What to do about them?
    I'll tell you what I do.
    I shut my eyes, and grit my teeth,
    And kinda muddle through!

2. Kaleidoscope: To make your own kaleidoscope, follow the directions given on pages 34 and 35 of Steven Caney's *Toy Book*. (See Bibliography/Caney.)

3. Symmetry: The patterns viewed through the kaleidoscope are usually symmetrical. *Symmetry* is the property that a figure has of corresponding in size, shape, and relative position of parts on opposite sides of a dividing line or median plane or about a center or axis. Having balanced proportions. A figure that is symmetrical can be folded in half so that both halves fit exactly. One half is a reflection of its other half. The parts of a figure on either side of a line of symmetry are congruent. A figure whose halves are reflections of each other are symmetric figures.

    For this activity you will need pattern blocks, (or something similar), 9 x 12 newsprint, scissors, crayons, tempera paint, graph paper. You may wish to take several days to complete this activity. Please follow the sequence.

    a) Get a sheet of paper and a pair of scissors. Cut out a paper heart. Did you first fold the paper? If so, why?

    Take another sheet of paper and a pair of scissors. Do not use a ruler, and do not make any measurements. Figure out a way to make the largest possible square from the piece of paper by making only one fold and only one cut.

    In both of these activities, the use of a line of symmetry was made. If the paper was folded to cut out the paper heart, two congruent parts were made, one on each side of the fold. After the square was cut out, and the paper opened, two congruent triangles may be seen, one on each side of the fold along a diagonal.

    b) Fold a piece of paper in half, and then place a drop of paint on the inside along the fold. Press the paper firmly together to scatter the paint. Unfold the paper. Does the fold separate the paint blot into two congruent parts?

    If a line through a plane figure is such that it separates the figure so that the part on one side is an exact reflection of the part on the other side, then the figure has a line of symmetry. The line that separates the figure is a line of symmetry. In this case, it is bilateral symmetry, for the two sides are congruent. To check it out,

24

place a mirror on the fold, (line of symmetry). Does the reflection in the mirror match the picture, and make a whole?

c) Cut out paper shapes for a square, circle, equilateral triangle, rectangle, and a regular hexagon.

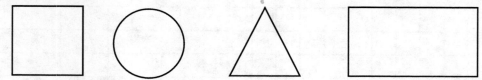

How many lines of symmetry can you make for each shape? Is there something special about the circle?

d) Use pattern blocks to make figures that are symmetrical. Show your figures to others, and have them show you the lines of symmetry. Can you make figures that have one, two, and/or more lines of symmetry? Try it!

Place the pattern blocks on a piece of paper, and trace around them. Cut along the outside edge of the picture that has been made. Can you fold the picture, to make a line of symmetry?

e) Draw a symmetric figure on the graph paper. Make a grid with two number lines that intersect at zero at right angles. Use ordered pairs of numbers, to locate points on the grid. The first number in an ordered pair tells the direction and distance from zero on the horizontal line. The second number tells the direction and distance from zero on the vertical line. Graph points on both sides of the axes to make symmetric shapes. (See following page.)

f) Look around. What can you find in the room, in the school, and outside that is symmetrical? Make a list. Can you locate the line of symmetry for one of the items on the list? Show others where it is. Is there agreement? Why? Why not?

g) Use two trapezoid pattern blocks. Make a shape that is a regular hexagon. Check it for shape by placing a hexagon pattern block on top of it. Does it fit? What fractional part is each trapezoid of the whole hexagon shape? *(It is one of the two parts, or one half.)* Use six triangle pattern blocks. Make a regular hexagon shape. Check it with the hexagon. What fractional part is each triangle of the whole hexagon shape? *(It is one of the six parts, or one-sixth of the whole.)* How many triangles make up one half of the hexagon shape? *(Three of the six triangles, three-sixths, make up one half of the hexagon shape.)* Depending upon the ability of the group, you may wish to do more fraction activities that include addition, subtraction, and multiplication.

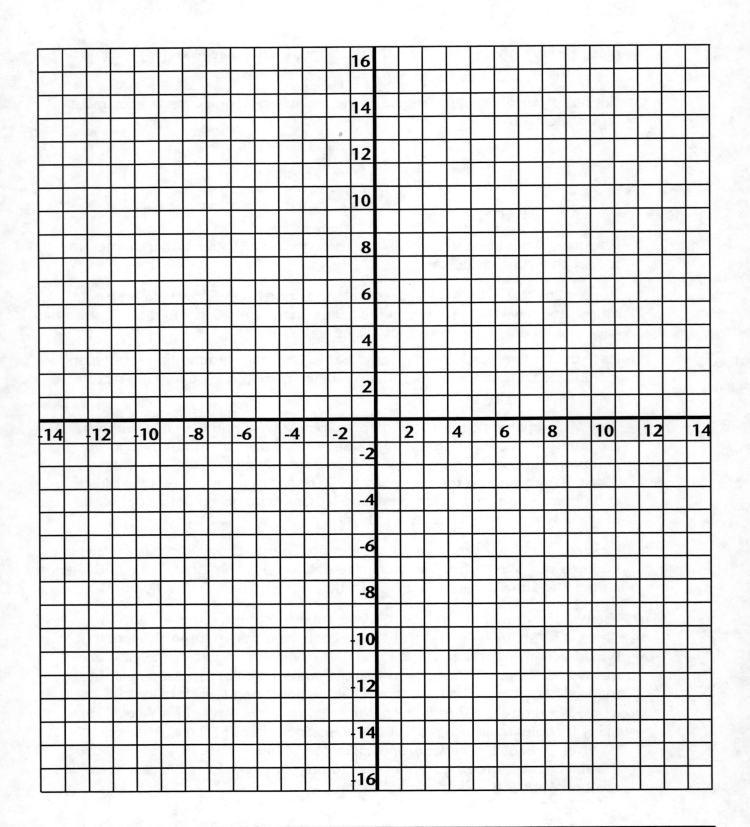

Origami Swan

You many use just about any kind of paper to make the swan: newspaper, typing paper, wrapping paper, recycled paper, foil-backed paper, or traditional origami paper. Thin, crisp paper gives the best results. The most important thing to remember in choosing paper is that the dimensions of the sheet should be exact. Measure to make sure that the sheet is precisely square. Trim if necessary. Make the creases carefully, matching corners where indicated. You may burnish folds with a thumbnail, a spoon, or any hard, smooth object. (For background information regarding origami, see Teacher Information section at the back of this guide.)

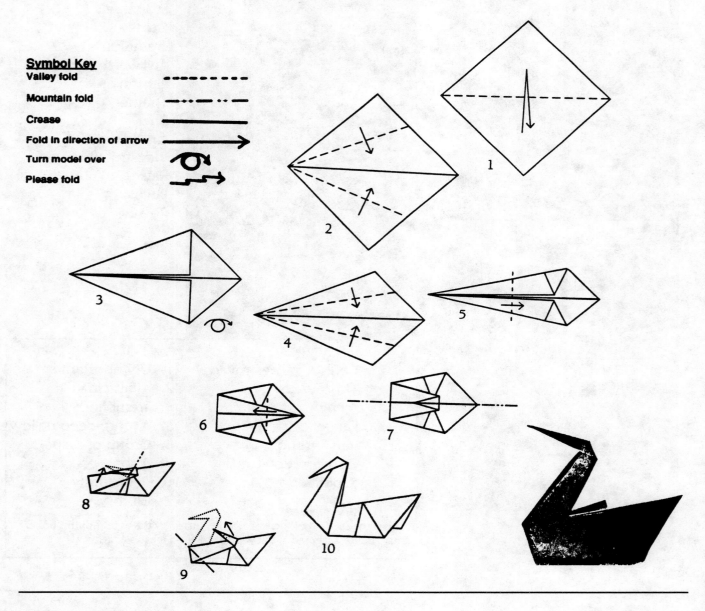

Symbol Key
Valley fold
Mountain fold
Crease
Fold in direction of arrow
Turn model over
Please fold

Crossword Puzzle One

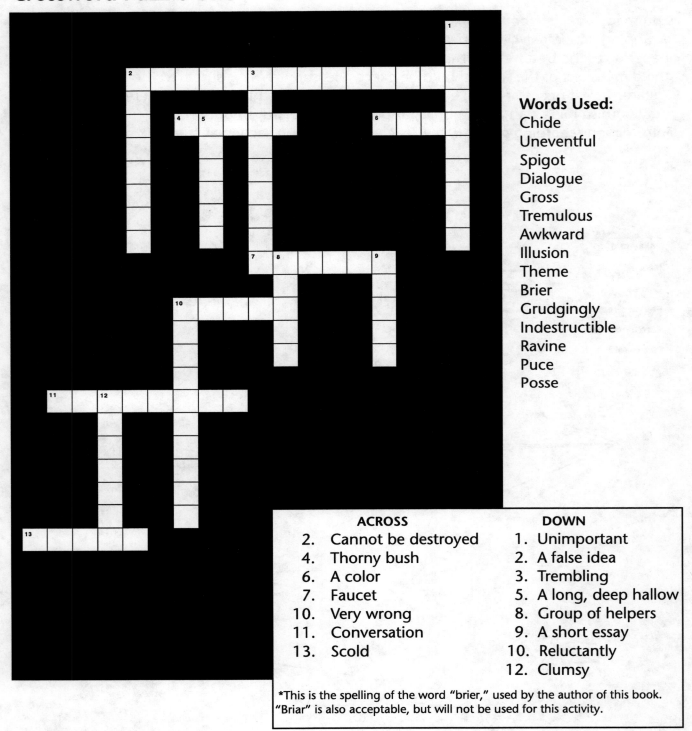

Words Used:
Chide
Uneventful
Spigot
Dialogue
Gross
Tremulous
Awkward
Illusion
Theme
Brier
Grudgingly
Indestructible
Ravine
Puce
Posse

ACROSS
2. Cannot be destroyed
4. Thorny bush
6. A color
7. Faucet
10. Very wrong
11. Conversation
13. Scold

DOWN
1. Unimportant
2. A false idea
3. Trembling
5. A long, deep hallow
8. Group of helpers
9. A short essay
10. Reluctantly
12. Clumsy

*This is the spelling of the word "brier," used by the author of this book. "Briar" is also acceptable, but will not be used for this activity.

Crossword Puzzle Two

Words Used:
Tormented
Remote
Accusation
Disappointment
Matador
Elongate
Silhouette
Obedient
Cascade
Rhododendron
Sustain
Anguish
Impetuously
Persist
Nauseated

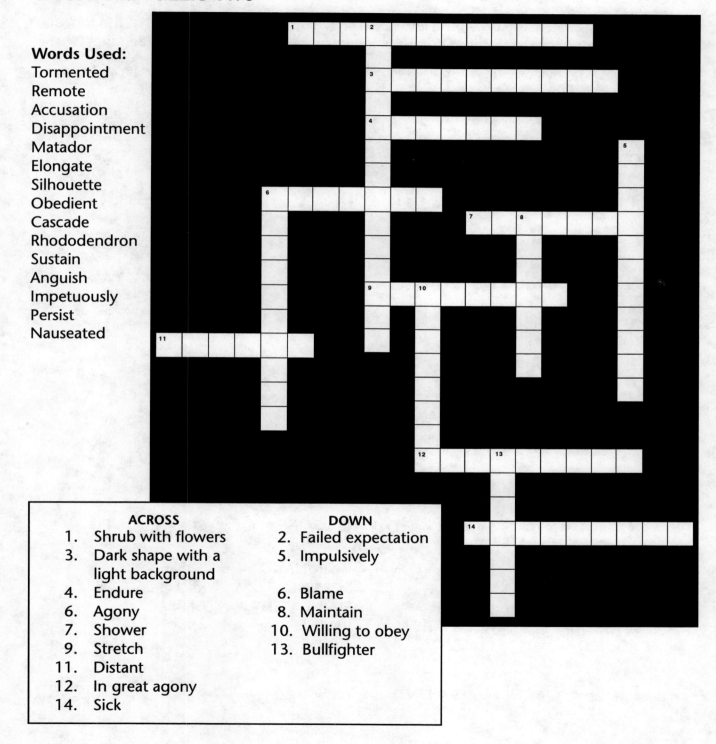

ACROSS
1. Shrub with flowers
3. Dark shape with a light background
4. Endure
6. Agony
7. Shower
9. Stretch
11. Distant
12. In great agony
14. Sick

DOWN
2. Failed expectation
5. Impulsively
6. Blame
8. Maintain
10. Willing to obey
13. Bullfighter

Word Search Puzzle One

Do the word search. Write down the letters that have not been used, starting at the top, and working left to right in each row. Group the letters into words to find the hidden message.

```
I  N  S  C  R  U  T  A  B  L  E  A
N  L  E  G  R  I  M  A  C  E  C  C
D  I  L  P  E  A  S  A  N  T  H  C
I  N  O  U  A  R  O  U  S  E  D  U
G  O  N  A  S  C  A  N  N  E  D  S
N  L  G  R  N  I  A  V  L  I  P  A
A  E  A  E  M  G  O  S  I  A  U  T
T  U  T  K  E  R  U  N  C  N  C  I
I  M  E  S  A  O  T  I  E  A  E  O
O  E  D  P  O  S  S  E  S  N  D  N
N  D  P  E  R  S  I  S  T  H  T  E
K  A  L  E  I  D  O  S  C  O  P  E
```

INSCRUTABLE	PUCE	INDIGNATION	POSSE
ILLUSION	CASCADE	SCANNED	KALEIDOSCOPE
LINOLEUMED	PERSIST	ELONGATED	GRIMACE
ANGUISH	ACCUSATION	RAVINE	
ROUSED	PEASANT	GROSS	

(Hidden Message: CHARLIE MAKES A TENT)

Word Search Puzzle Two

Do the word search. Write down the letters that have not been used, starting at the top, and working left to right in each row. Group the letters into words to find the hidden message.

```
E   M   P   H   A   T   I   C   A   L   L   Y
X   I   M   P   E   T   U   O   U   S   L   Y
A   N   N   R   E   V   E   N   G   E   S   A
G   C   P   C   H   R   S   P   I   G   O   T
G   I   M   A   R   Y   B   R   I   E   R   R
E   D   A   F   T   E   T   H   E   M   E   E
R   E   T   L   A   H   D   H   H   A   S   M
A   N   A   A   A   N   E   I   M   U   N   U
T   T   D   I   H   A   P   T   B   I   P   L
E   Y   O   L   S   U   M   M   I   L   C   O
D   E   R   C   H   I   D   E   R   C   E   U
H   O   P   E   L   E   S   S   N   E   S   S
```

EMPHATICALLY	SPIGOT	PATHETIC	FLAIL
INCREDIBLE	BRIER*	TREMULOUS	MATADOR
IMPETUOUSLY	CHIDE	THEME	INCIDENT
HOPELESSNESS	EXAGGERATED	REVENGE	RHYTHMIC

Note: This is the spelling of the word "brier" used by the author in this book. "Briar" is acceptable, but will not be used for this activity.

(Hidden Message: SARA HAS AN UNHAPPY SUMMER)

Teacher Information

Glossary of Words About Mental Retardation and Learning:

Abstract: An idea that is not based upon or easily verifiable through the five senses. Ideas about love, death, and loyalty are abstract.

Concept: An idea or thought.

Concrete: Something that can be perceived through the senses. A picture of a dog is concrete. The way a dog smells is concrete.

Developmental Disability: A kind of disability that limits how much a person will learn and how fast he or she will develop. Mental retardation is a developmental disability.

Early Intervention: The practice of educating children from the time somebody notices their disability, if possible right after birth. The idea behind the practice is that valuable learning time is lost if therapies and programs for learning are delayed until a child would normally start school. Children who receive early intervention start school with more of the skills of other children their age.

Expressive Language: The kind of language we use to express our thoughts and feelings to others.

Intelligence: One measure of our ability to learn and to think. Intelligence is measured by tests that may or may not give a full picture of our abilities.

Intelligence Quotient: Also called IQ, the number a person is given after tests that measure the ability to learn. The average IQ is 100.

Mainstreaming: Teaching children with disabilities and nondisabled children together. Mainstreaming is sometimes called integration. It replaced the older system which put children with disabilities in classes and schools by themselves. All children today can learn more about themselves and others by sharing the same classroom.

Mental Retardation: A permanent condition that causes persons to learn more slowly than others and usually limits their level of understanding. A person who is mentally retarded will be slow to develop in all areas, both mental and physical.

Motivation: Something besides a task itself that inspires someone to do something. Praise and rewards for success are motivators. Punishment for failure is a motivator, too, but it is not as effective.

Receptive Language: The language that we understand when we hear someone else speaking or when we read.

John Newbery:

John Newbery was born on July 19, 1713, in the village of Waltham St. Lawrence, Berkshire, England. His father was a farmer. However, an ancestor, Ralph Newbery, had been a publisher, and when John went to work, it was in a newspaper and printing business. After his master's death, John married the man's widow. She had three children, and three more children were born to her and Newbery. In 1744

Newbery opened his own shop in London, at the sign of the *Bible and Crown*. Before long he moved to St. Paul's Churchyard, at the sign of the *Bible and Sun*. Here he published many books for children and adults, writing some of them himself. He died on December 22, 1767, at the age of 54. The epitaph on his grave describes "the humble wisdom that...teaches moral lessons to the rising generation." His son Francis followed him in the business, and published many books for children.

Swan Lake:

Background: This theme was popular at the time in Germany, and provided the basis for Peter Tchaikovsky's first ballet, commissioned by the Russian Imperial Theatre. The composer began his work in August of 1875, and finished it in April of 1876. When presented for the first time, it received a mixed reception. The music was said to be monotonous and boring. It was to be 13 years before the composer wrote another ballet. *Swan Lake* was not seen in its present form until 1895, when Tchaikovsky was already dead. The ballet was subsequently given a new ending for the Bolshoi Theatre, in which good triumphed over evil. The final scene, in which the Prince fights the wicked wizard, now provides one of the most dramatic dances in the entire ballet.

Synopsis: The story of Swan Lake concerns a widowed queen who has but one child, a son, Prince Siegfried, who prefers hunting in the forest to a quiet life at home. When he comes of age, the Prince is ordered by his mother to wed. She arranges a birthday ball for the Prince, inviting the daughters from the richest families in the land, and princesses from over the sea.

Enjoying the days before the ball, the Prince goes hunting once again, and sees some beautiful swans on the lake. Enamored of the one seeming to wear a golden crown, he follows it to a ruined castle. As darkness comes, the Prince sees a beautiful maiden. She tells the Prince of the spell cast upon her by the wicked wizard, explaining that only a promise of everlasting love could break the spell, compelling her to be a swan during the daylight hours. The Prince declares his love for Odette, as she vanishes in the mist.

The night of the ball, the wicked wizard arrives accompanied by his daughter Odile, who has taken on the appearance of Odette. The prince, thinking that this is Odette, declares his everlasting love and tells the queen of his intention to marry. All the while, the Prince has not noticed a swan beating its wings against a window. As the Prince swears to love no other, there is a crash of thunder as the wizard and his daughter disappear into the night.

Realizing that he has been tricked, the Prince rushes out to the swan, begging forgiveness. However, the swan has vanished into the gloom. The Prince dashes into the woods. There he sees the swan girls, and finds Odette standing alone, head bent in sorrow. Losing the will to live, Odette sinks to the ground. The wicked wizard appears in the form of a giant owl, and a struggle to the death begins with the saddened Prince. The Prince finally tears off the wings of the owl, draining the wizard of his power. The wizard soon dies, and Odette revives, as the power of Love overcomes the force of Evil.

Swans:

Swans, geese, and ducks belong to the same bird family. They have in common flat beaks, short legs, webbed feet, short tails, and long necks. All are at home on the water. They use their beaks to smooth and oil their feathers, to keep them waterproof. There are seven kinds of swans.

The mute swans, originally found in Europe, were introduced in North America as decorative birds. In fact, many of the mutes in England are true blue bloods whose ancestry can be traced at least 700 years. The English developed an elaborate system of marking birds and maintaining a swan-roll of ownership. Swan-marks could be inherited, willed, or sold. Distinctive swan-marks were owned by individuals, colleges, hospitals, religious orders, towns, officials, guilds, and manors as well as commercial companies. The swans have bright orange bills and the adult males have a prominent black knob connecting the top of the bill to the forehead. Mutes hold their necks in a characteristic S-curve, with their bills pointed down. Most mute swans don't breed until they are four years old. However, some pairs will establish and defend a territory for two years or more before they breed.

Two native swans of North America are the trumpeter and the whistling swans, named for their cries. The trumpeter is North America's largest native waterfowl, weighing 21-30 pounds, and standing four feet tall. Its beak is pink at birth, then turns solid black during the first winter.

All swans are powerful flyers, some with a wing span of six feet and a speed of forty or more miles an hour. They usually build nests near the water, sometimes on small islands. The nest is very large, at times being 9 to 12 feet across, and 3 feet deep, and is made up of cattails, sticks, and other vegetation. It is often built on top of muskrat houses. Eggs hatch in 28 to 32 days, somewhat longer for the mute swan, (35 days after the last egg is laid), the average clutch size being six eggs. Young swans, called cygnets, hatch with bodies protected by a warm coat of soft gray down. They are independent, knowing how to swim as soon as they are hatched, and soon feed themselves on insects and small crustaceans, although as adults they are usually vegetarians.

Although wild swans have few natural predators, they have been killed by hunters and disease. Once listed in the United States as an endangered species, the trumpeter swan now appears to have escaped extinction.

Black swans live in Australia and New Zealand. They are about as big as mute swans. Each wing has a white band along the back edge. Otherwise, the plumage is all black. They live in very large groups, sometimes as many as 50,000 in one flock. Black-necked swans live in South America. They have pink legs and feet, and a call that is weak and sounds like a toy trumpet. Coscoroba swans, also living in South America, have pink legs and feet. They are small, with white plumage with black tips on the wings. They look more like geese than swans.

Some swans migrate very long distances, and in clear weather may fly as high as 5,000 feet. They will travel mainly at night, stopping to rest and feed during the day. Mute swan populations are concentrated in New York, Connecticut, Rhode Island, Michigan, Minnesota, Wisconsin, and Illinois. Atlantic coast flocks now number about 10,000 birds, and are growing at an astounding rate of 30% a year. The rapid growth concerns wildlife biologists, ornithologists, and naturalists, for large numbers of birds eating large amounts of aquatic vegetation can drastically change wetland wildlife and the marshes themselves. Mute swans eat about nine pounds of vegetation a day, even more in icy weather. Removing this much plant life considerably cuts habitat and food resources for native waterfowl, fish, and other aquatic life.

West Virginia:

Nickname:	The Mountain State
Capital:	Charleston
State bird:	Cardinal
State flower:	Rhododendron
State tree:	Sugar Maple
State animal:	Black Bear
State fish:	Brook Trout
State colors:	Blue and gold
State motto:	Mountaineers are always free. *Montani Semper Liberi*
State song:	*The West Virginia Hills; This Is My West Virginia; West Virginia, My Home Sweet Home*
Statehood:	June 20, 1863, the 35th state
Area:	24,181 square miles; 41st in size among the states
Borders:	Ohio on the northwest, Pennsylvania and Maryland on the north, Virginia on the east and south, Kentucky on the southwest
Origin of Name:	West Virginia was formed from the western counties of the state of Virginia, which was named for Elizabeth, the Virgin Queen of England

Origami:

In the 6th century A.D., Buddhist monks traveling to Japan brought along a new product manufactured in China. The Japanese called the thin, flat sheets of plant fiber *kami*, meaning "paper." Shortly thereafter, folding squares of paper into stylized representations of animals and people became a national tradition. Origami figures were crafted for ceremonies, home decorations, and toys.

The oldest origami designs consisted of a few simple, easily remembered folds. Mothers taught their daughters the folding patterns, and in this way the art of origami was passed down through the generations, not by written record, but through memory.

Magic and mathematics revolutionized the ancient art in the 20th century. *Houdini's Paper Magic*, published in 1922, introduced professional and amateur magicians to origami. They, in turn, intrigued audiences around the world with the mysteries of paper folding. More recently, engineers and mathematicians have applied their disciplines to paper. Starting with rectangular or polygonal sheets instead of the traditional square, they fold intricate designs with hundreds of creases and create three dimensional, multifaceted figures.

Paper folding achieved widespread popularity in the 1950s and 1960s, thanks to folders Akira Yoshizawa of Japan, Robert Harbin of England, and Samuel Randlett of the United States. The three developed a universal code of dots, dashes, and arrows to represent folds.

Recipes From Southern West Virginia

Fruit Cream Salad

2 small boxes orange-flavored gelatin   1 -6 oz. can cherries, drained and cut
2 cups boiling water   1-20 oz. can crushed pineapple
1 pint vanilla ice cream   1 cup pecans

Dissolve gelatin in boiling water. Add ice cream and stir until it is melted. Add cherries, pineapple and nuts. Store in the refrigerator.

Macaroni Salad

2 cups cooked macaroni, strained   1 cut up green pepper
    under cold water and drained   1 cut up tomato
2 tablespoons sweet pickle juice   1 cut up cucumber
Salt and pepper

Mix all of the ingredients together.

Orange Salad

1 large, or 2 small, jars of pineapple-orange jelly
1 can crushed pineapple, drained
1 can mandarin oranges

Stir well together, and add:

1 cup cool whip
1 cup small curd cottage cheese

Stir well and chill.

Lemon Bars

1 box yellow cake mix
1 egg
1 stick melted margarine

Mix above ingredients together and press in a greased 13 x 9 inch glass dish.

Mix together: 1 pound box confectioners sugar
    2 eggs
    1-8 oz. cream cheese
    2 tablespoons lemon flavor

Spread evenly over ingredients in glass dish. Bake 35 minutes in glass dish in a 350° oven.

Bibliography

Mental Retardation:

Baroff, George. *Mental Retardation: Nature, Cause, and Management.* Washington, DC: Hemisphere, 1986.

Bergman, Thomas. *We Laugh, We Love, We Cry.* Milwaukee, WI: Gareth Stevens Children's Books, 1989.

Cleaver, Vera. *Me Too.* Philadelphia, PA: Lippincott, 1973.

Drew, Clifford. *Mental Retardation: A Life Cycle Approach.* St.Louis, MO: Times Mirror/Mosby College, 1984.

Dunbar, Robert. *Mental Retardation.* NY: A Venture Book/Watts, 1991.

Forrai, Maria. *A Look At Mental Retardation.* Minneapolis, MN: Lerner Publications, 1976.

Hall, Lynn. *Just One Friend.* NY: Collier Books, 1988, 1985. (paperback)

Hall, Lynn. *Just One Friend.* NY: Scribners, 1985.

Litchfield, Ada. *Making Room For Uncle Joe.* Niles, IL: Whitman, 1984.

Long, Judy. *Volunteer Spring.* NY: Dodd, Mead, 1976.

Smith, Doris. *Kelly's Creek.* NY: Crowell, 1975.

Smith, John David. *Minds Made Feeble: The Kallikaks.* Rockville, MD: Aspen Systems, 1985.

Westling, David. *Introduction to Mental Retardation.* Englewood Cliffs, NJ: Prentice-Hall, 1986.

Swans:

Althea. *Swans.* Chicago, IL: Longman Group USA, 1988.

Coldrey, Jennifer. *The Swan On The Lake.* Milwaukee, WI: G. Stevens, 1986.

Coldrey, Jennifer. *The World Of Swans.* Milwaukee, WI: G. Stevens, 1986.

Featherly, Jay. *Ko-hah: The Call Of The Trumpeter Swan.* Minneapolis, MN: Carolrhoda Books, 1986.

Fegely, Thomas. *Wonders of Geese and Swans.* NY: Dodd, Mead Company, 1976.

Horton, Tom. *Swanfall: Journey of the Tundra Swans.* NY: Walker, 1991.

Hutchins, Ross. *The Last Trumpeters.* Chicago, IL: Rand McNally, 1967.

King, Deborah. *Swan.* NY: Lothrop, Lee & Shepard, 1985.

Mason, Edwin. *Swans and Wild Geese.* Chicago, IL: Follett, 1970.

Scott, Jack. *Swans.* NY: Putnam, 1987.

Selsam, Millicent. *A First Look at Ducks, Geese, and Swans.* NY: Walker, 1990.

Wilmore, Sylvia. *Swans of the World.* NY: Taplinger Publishing Company, 1974.

Swan Lake:
Diamond, Donna. *Swan Lake.* NY: Holiday House, 1980.

Helprin, Mark. *Swan Lake.* Boston: Houghton Mifflin, 1989.

Isadora, Rachel. *Swan Lake.* NY: G.P. Putnam's Sons, 1989.

West Virginia:
Aylesworth, Thomas. *Atlantic: District of Columbia, Virginia, West Virginia.* NY: Chelsea House, 1988.

Aylesworth, Thomas. *Atlantic: District of Columbia, Virginia, West Virginia.* NY: Chelsea House, 1991.

Fradin, Dennis. *West Virginia in Words and Pictures.* Chicago, IL: Children's Press, 1980.

Stein, R. Conrad. *West Virginia.* Chicago, IL: Children's Press, 1990.

Thompson, Kathleen. *West Virginia.* Milwaukee, WI: Raintree Publishers, 1988.

Sign Language:
Baker-Shenk, Charlotte Lee. *American Sign Language: A Teacher's Resource Text On Grammar and Culture.* Washington, DC: Clerc Books, 1991.

Bornstein, Harry. *Nursery Rhymes From Mother Goose: Told in Signed English.* Washington, DC: Kendall Green Publications, 1992.

Bourke, Linda. *Handmade ABC: A Manual Alphabet.* Reading, MA: Addison-Wesley, 1981.

Chaplin, Susan. *I Can Sign My ABCs.* Washington, DC: Kendall Green Publications, 1986.

Eastman, Gilbert. *From Mime to Sign.* Silver Spring, MD: T.J. Publishers, 1989.

Fant, Louie. *Intermediate Sign Language.* Northridge, CA: Joyce Media, 1980.

Gillen, Patricia. *My Signing Book of Numbers.* Washington, DC: Kendall Green Publications, 1988.

Greene, Laura. *Sign Language Talk.* NY: Franklin Watts, 1988.

Greene, Laura. *Discovering Sign Language.* Washington, DC: Green Publications, 1988.

Hafer, Jan Christian. *Signing For Reading Success.* Washington, DC: Kendell Green Publications, 1986.

Hoemann, Harry. *I Want To Talk: A Child Model of American Sign Language.* Silver Spring, MD: National Association of the Deaf, 1980.

Hoemann, Harry. *Introduction to American Sign Language.* Bowling Green, OH: Bowling Green Press, 1986.

Neisser, Arden. *The Other Side Of Silence: Sign Language and the Deaf Community in America.* NY: Knopf, 1983.

Newell, William. *B.A.S.I.C. S.I.G.N. Communication.* Silver Spring, MD: National Association of the Deaf, 1983.

Riekehof, Lottie. *The Joy Of Signing: The Illustrated Guide For Mastering Sign Language and the Manual Alphabet.* Springfield, MO: Gospel Publishing House, 1987.

Other:

Caney, Steven. *Toy Book*. NY: Workman Publishing Company, 1972. Pages 34 and 35

Dakos, Kalli. *If You're Not Here, Please Raise Your Hand: Poems About School*. NY: Four Winds/Macmillan, 1990.

dePaola, Tomie. *Tomie dePaola's Book of Poems*. NY: G. Putnam, 1988. Page 81

Livingston, Myra Cohn. *Remembering and Other Poems*. NY: Margaret K. McElderry Books, 1989. Page 48

Merriam, Eve. *Jamboree*. NY: A Yearling Book/Dell, 1984. Page 26

Prelutsky, Jack, selected by. *The Random House Book of Poetry*. NY: Random House, 1983. Page 33

Audio-Visual Bibliography

Coldrey, Jennifer. *The World Of Swans*. (Filmstrip) Milwaukee, WI: G. Stevens Media, 1987.

Keyes, Daniel. *Charly*. (Videorecording) NY: CBS/Fox Video, 1989. Rated PG.*(Charly, a gentle retarded man, is befriended by his night school teacher, who persuades a famous clinic to do experimental neurosurgery on him to improve his learning capabilities. The results are spectacular at first, and Charly learns also to handle his emotional growth. However, he must soon deal with a frightening discovery. This is based on the book Flowers for Algernon.)*

Maas, J.B., Producer. *Bravo Gloria!* (Videorecording) Ithaca, NY: Cornell University, Psychology Film Unit, 1988. *(Gloria Lehnoff is 32 years old, but has the mental development of a 12 year old. However, Gloria leads a productive and rewarding life, working in a sheltered workshop, volunteering in a preschool and serving as assistant cantor in her synagogue.)*

Shapiro, Eric, Director. *The Fragile X Mystery*. (Videorecording) South Burlington, VT: Ambose Video Publishing, 1990. *(Discusses the broken chromosome which causes a type of inherited mental retardation called fragile X syndrome. People with fragile X syndrome and their relatives are interviewed. Includes a discussion of the way in which scientists are trying to find a method to prevent this syndrome from occurring. Originally broadcast as an episode of the television program 48 Hours on September 29, 1990.)*

Tchaikovsky, Peter Ilyich. *Swan Lake*. (Videorecording/106 min.) NY: PolyGram Records, distributor, 1987. (Originally recorded in 1966, starring Rudolf Nureyev, Margot Fonteyn, Wiener Staatsopernballett.)

Tchaikovsky, Peter Ilyich. *Swan Lake*. (Videorecording/126 min.) Sea Bright, NJ: Kultur, 1984. (Gene Kelly, narrator. Starring Natalia Bessmertnova, Alexander Bogatyrev, Bolshoi Ballet Company.)

Tchaikovsky, Peter Ilyich. *Swan Lake*. (Story Sound Recording/Margot Fonteyn) Orlando, FL: Harcourt Brace Jovanovich, 1991, 1976.

Tchaikovsky, Peter Ilyich. *Swan Lake*. (Story Sound Recording/Cassette/Clare Bloom) NY: Caedmon, 1981.

Tchaikovsky, Peter Ilyich. *Swan Lake*. (Music Sound Recording/Cassette) London: Audio Fidelity.

Tchaikovsky, Peter Ilyich. *Swan Lake*. (Music Sound Recording/Compact Disc) Hamburg, Germany: Deutsche Grammophon.

Tchaikovsky, Peter Ilyich. *Swan Lake*. (Music Sound Recording/Compact Disc) NY: RCA Victor Red Seal, 1989.

Tchaikovsky, Peter Ilyich. *Swan Lake.* (Music Sound Recording/Compact Disc) Universal City, CA: MCA Records, 1988.

Turner Program Services, Inc. *West Virginia.* (Videorecording/VHS) Milwaukee, WI: Raintree Publishers, 1988.

Audio-Visual Bibliography/Sign Language

Altfeld, Sheldon. *The Sign of Our Times.* (Videorecording) North Hollywood, CA: All Occasion Video, 1986. (Program is in American Sign Language, normal sound, and open captions.)

Barry, Mike. *I Want To Talk.* (Videorecording) Bowling Green, IN: Bowling Green State University: WBGU-TV Learning Services, 1980.

Costello, Elaine. *Say It By Signing.* (Videorecording) NY: Crown Video, 1985.

Seago, Billy, told by. *The Magic Pot: Signed English.* (Videorecording) Seattle, WA: Sign-A-Vision, 1987.

Seago, Billy, told by. T*he House That Jack Built: American Sign Language.* (Videorecording) Seattle, WA: Sign-A-Vision, 1987.

Smith, Cheryl, et. al. *Signing Naturally. Level 1. Student Videotext.* (Videorecording) Berkeley, CA: Dawn Sign Press, 1988. (American Sign Language Series)

Vogel, Carole. *Strangers: Stranger Dangers.* (Videorecording) Jacksonville, IL: Illinois School for the Deaf, 1989.

Word Search Answers

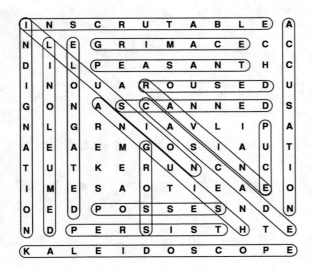

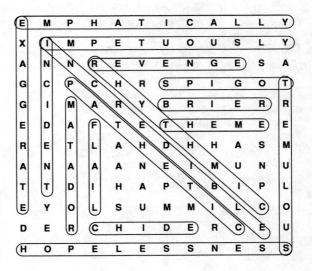

Crossword Puzzle Answers

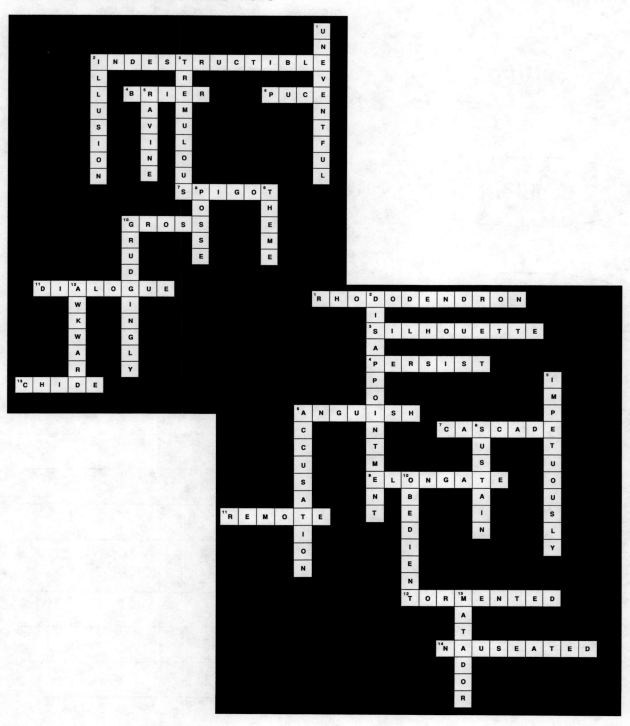

Story Map

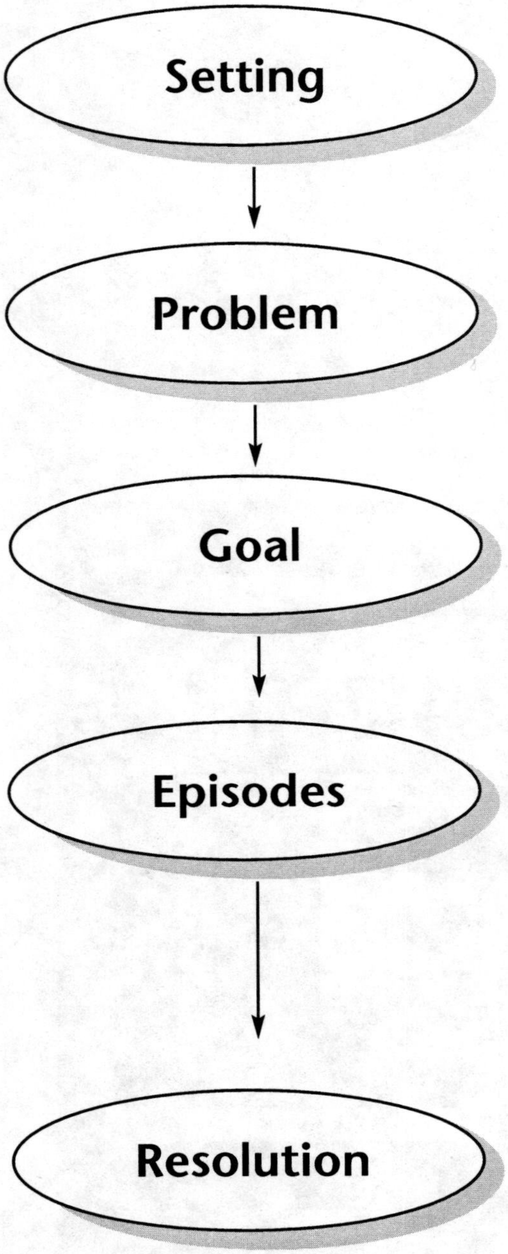

Setting

↓

Problem

↓

Goal

↓

Episodes

↓

Resolution

Characters_____

_____

Time and Place_____

_____

Problem_____

_____

_____

Goal_____

_____

_____

Beginning ⟶ Development ⟶ Outcome

_____

_____

_____

_____

Resolution_____

_____

_____

_____

Using Character Webs—In the Novel Unit Approach

Attribute Webs are simply a visual representation of a character from the novel. They provide a systematic way for the students to organize and recap the information they have about a particular character. Attribute webs may be used after reading the novel to recapitulate information about a particular character or completed gradually as information unfolds, done individually, or finished as a group project.

One type of character attribute web uses these divisions:

● How a character acts and feels. (How does the character feel in this picture? How would you feel if this happened to you? How do you think the character feels?)

● How a character looks. (Close your eyes and picture the character. Describe him to me.)

● Where a character lives. (Where and when does the character live?)

● How others feel about the character. (How does another specific character feel about our character?)

In group discussion about the student attribute webs and specific characters, the teacher can ask for backup proof from the novel. You can also include inferential thinking.

Attribute webs need not be confined to characters. They may also be used to organize information about a concept, object or place.

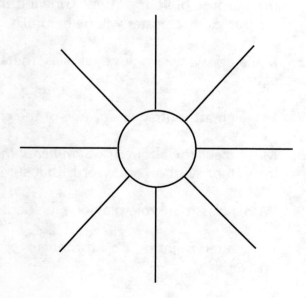

ASSESSMENT FOR *THE SUMMER OF THE SWANS*

Assessment is an on-going process, more than a quiz at the end of the book. Points may be added to show the level of achievement. When an item is completed, the teacher and the student check it.

Name _____ Date _____

Student   **Teacher**

_____   _____   1.   Make a story map.

_____   _____   2.   Give yourself one point for each vocabulary activity successfully completed.

_____   _____   3.   Write chapter titles that indicate something that might happen or to create suspense to encourage the reader.

_____   _____   4.   Write a letter to an advice columnist in the local paper. You may take the role of Sara, or you may take a different part and have different problems. Explain your problem(s) to the columnist and ask for some specific advice.

_____   _____   5.   Create a poster about Charlie and his disappearance. What is the purpose of your poster? Knowing that, what will you include, so the poster will be helpful?

_____   _____   6.   Make up two examples of similes, metaphors, and/or personification.

_____   _____   7.   Make an attribute web for one of the characters in the novel.

_____   _____   8.   Make a collage about *The Summer of the Swans*. Include important symbols and words that summarize the story.

_____   _____   9.   With a classmate role play one incident in the story.

_____   _____   10.   Write a ten point quiz on this novel for a classmate. Make an answer key.

_____